Choosi

Titles in the Christian Counselling Series

The Challenge of Singleness *Trevor J. Partridge*
Choosing Your Vocation *Trevor J. Partridge*
Discovering Your Place in the Body of Christ
Selwyn Hughes
Fifteen Ways to a More Effective Prayer Life
Selwyn Hughes
Seven Steps to Overcoming Depression
Selwyn Hughes
Ten Principles for a Happy Marriage
Selwyn Hughes

Choosing Your Vocation

Trevor J. Partridge

Marshalls

Marshalls Paperbacks
Marshall Morgan & Scott
1 Bath Street, London EC1V 9LB

First published by Marshall Morgan & Scott 1982

ISBN: 0 551 00959 4

Printed in Great Britain by
Richard Clay (The Chaucer Press) Ltd,
Bungay, Suffolk

Contents

Preface

The books in the *Christian Counselling Series* are written with two main groups of people in mind. The first group are those who facing a personal problem look for something concise and readable that speaks to their need. The second group are ministers and counsellors who wish to place in the hands of people seeking help something that will supplement their own individual counselling efforts.

The authors, writing from their own personal encounters with people who have faced the problems listed in this series, do so with a good deal of confidence. They claim that when the principles outlined in these books have been followed they have contributed in a positive manner to helping people resolve their difficulties. The content is firmly based on Scripture, but the authors in their writing seek to apply Biblical principles in such a way that helps readers, not only to know what they should do but how to do it.

Introduction

The purpose of this book is to bring into focus the factors that need to be taken into account when considering a vocation. It is designed to help you think through prayerfully and carefully God's will as it relates to your life's work, and to follow some practical exercises to help you narrow the field of opportunities that may be open to you. It is designed specifically for those who have a personal faith in God through Christ, and are committed to seeking his purposes for their life. Although teaching concerning the will of God is quite prevalent in the Church, very often the specific area of choosing a life vocation has been neglected or at best left to secular career officers for guidance. This book is not designed to be extensive or conclusive, but to give pointers in considering the direction of one's life work.

Why work?

'I just feel so frustrated. I'm earning a good wage, I have a lovely wife and family, but I feel so unfulfilled at work.' John, a bright, intelligent man in his mid-thirties was finding he couldn't concentrate on his work; it had become a laborious chore to go to the office each day. He had done little or no planning when thinking of a career and now he was finding no fulfilment or satisfaction in his job so that he had reached the point of considering changing it.

Bill was also like this. He was always the joker at school. He never took his studies seriously and failed his exams. 'It's alright,' he laughed when he got his exam results, 'I'll be an artist and draw the dole.' But deep down inside he was worried about his future. He found a job driving a lorry but only a short time went by before he married and children were on the way. He became bored with driving. His mind was active and he felt frustrated. 'If only I'd given more thought to a vocation,' he told himself, 'life would have more meaning.'

Choosing a vocation and making a decision about our life's work is a major step, which determines the course and quality of our life. Choices have to be given some serious thought, as wise decisions about our aims in life have to be arrived at.

In choosing a vocation we must ask the basic question: why do we work? To eat, to live, to earn a wage? No, we work because God created us to be achievers – to do something worthwhile with our lives, something that is meaningful and productive. Many people develop deep frustrations and a failure complex, because they have never really found anything that they can do well, that brings meaning and satisfaction to them. They end up doing a job that they dislike, that carries no job satisfaction, and this affects the quality of the rest of their life.

In a research that Dr Paul Tournier conducted he discovered that most people do not love their work and many become disenchanted with it. Bruce Carlson in his book *Dare to live now* says, 'If you are miserable or bored in your work, or dread going to it . . . then God is speaking to you. He either wants you to change the job you are in, or more likely he wants to change you.' We must never see our vocation just as an economic necessity for survival; God has much more in life for us than that. God is not in the business of humdrum routine, but in bringing a sense of purpose and destiny into our lives, so that they will count for him. On the other hand, our vocation must never be deified or held in such an exalted position that it dominates and constricts our life. Our vocation must bring to our lives a sense of dignified significance in the plans and purposes of God. Dorothy Sayers in *Creed or Chaos* says of work that it is 'a way of life in which the nature of man should find its proper exercise and delight, and so fulfil itself to the glory of God.'

When we were created in the image of God, he dropped within us that creative drive that finds its fulfilment through a meaningful vocation. Yet so often in the Church we neglect to help people discover the vocation of his choosing and so many of the lives of God's people are not enriched but impoverished, from the frustration and unfulfilment they experience every day of their lives. The discovery of God's purpose for our lives is one of the greatest factors in leading a meaningful and productive Christian life.

How can we begin to discover the area of vocation to which God is calling us? We must first of all come in an attitude of prayer and openness to him, seeking his guidance, dedicating ourselves to him, and telling him that we wish to discover his purposes. 'I beseech you, therefore, brethren by the mercies of God that you present your bodies a living sacrifice, holy, acceptable unto God which is your reasonable service' (Romans 12.1). Then, pray every day for guidance about your career, affirming that God has a purpose for your life and that you are on the road towards discovering it.

Finding our identity

Throughout life each one of us develops a self-image based on the reflections, opinions and judgments of others. It has its beginnings in the early, formative years of our life as our natural abilities and aptitudes are beginning to emerge. In these developing years, the identity we begin to create for ourselves is crucial, colouring and flavouring our motivation, thoughts and feelings about everything else and setting the stage for what we do and become in later life. If we develop a negative self-image, the insecurity and inferiority that accompany it can affect our vocational choice. Poor or unwise vocational choices are made, which set us on a miserable road to frustration and unfulfilment. So often during these years we accept the values and judgments that others place on us, rather than recognising and considering God's will and purpose for our lives. If we do not discover and move into his vocational purposes for us, we become frustrated and develop feelings of insecurity.

Realising that we are unique in God's sight and that he has a specific plan for our life is one of the most exciting aspects of the Christian life and the greatest influencing factor to personal achievement. Just as there are no two snow flakes or blades of grass that are the same, so it is with us. There is no one else just like us, and God has a revelation of himself to present through us that he can accomplish through no one else: a life message to paint on the canvas of our life through the plan and purpose and vocation of his choosing. 'You made all the delicate, inner parts of my body, and knit them together in my mother's womb. Thank you for making me so wonderfully complex! It is amazing to think about. Your workmanship is marvellous – and how well I know it. You were there while I was being formed in utter seclusion! You saw me before I was born and scheduled each day of my life before I began to breathe. Every day was recorded in your Book! How precious it is, Lord, to realize that you are thinking about me constantly! I can't even count how many times a day your thoughts turn towards me. And when I waken in the morning, you are still thinking of me!' (Psalm 139.13–18, T.L.B.).

Develop a healthy self respect for the abilities and aptitudes he has given you. You are made in the image of God. He doesn't despise and denigrate you, so don't allow yourself to be overcome by self-pity concerning strengths and abilities you feel you don't have, but begin to place on yourself the value and worth he places on you. You may be of a shy, retiring and introverted disposition, the kind of person who is even nervous of his own shadow. But remember, as we bring our weaknesses to God, he will turn them into his strengths. 'My strength is made perfect in your weakness' (2 Corinthians 12.9).

'For ye see your calling, brethren, how that not many wise men after the flesh, not many mighty, not many noble, are called: but God hath chosen the foolish things of the world to confound the wise; and God hath chosen the weak things of the world to confound the things which are mighty; and base things of the world, and things which are despised, hath God chosen, yea, and things which are not, to bring to nought things that are' (1 Corinthians 1.26–28).

Recognise that God does not love us for what we do in life but for who we are, and that because of who we are, he has a specific purpose for us to fulfil. When we become secure in that love we can say with the Apostle Paul, 'For I have learned in whatsoever state I am therewith to be content' (Philippians 4.11).

A well-known Bible commentator put it like

this: 'Consider the fact that you are "custom made" by God, heredity and environment – all factors contributing to making you – were governed by the Creator. All of this was done because you are designed to fulfil a specific purpose in history – a purpose no one else can completely fulfil. The fulfilment of this ultimate purpose is left within your power. It depends on the way you respond to your Creator.'

Vocational adjustment

Many people go through life like square pegs in round holes. They are frustrated and unfulfilled because early in life they made the wrong vocational choice. There are several reasons why people are motivated to choose the wrong vocations.

1. *No clear guidance.* Many people just drift into a career. They are not sure what they want to do in life. They have no clear sense of direction and purpose. They receive no vocational counselling and just accept the first opportunity of earning a living that comes along.

2. *Circumstances.* Often the circumstances of home and family prevent them from pursuing the opportunities of further education. Family pressures and commitments necessitate that they find work to provide financial support for their family.

3. *Panic.* Because there has been no planning and little thought given to vocation, people find themselves leaving school without the necessary

qualifications. Therefore they panic and accept the first offer that comes along because they are afraid that nothing else will turn up for them. They then find themselves trapped on a treadmill of unfulfilment and frustration.

4. *Parental influence.* Parents often decide what is the best vocation for their children, and although this can be very helpful, sometimes it is not realistic. Often parents are frustrated because they were unable to pursue the vocation of their choosing. When a child comes into the family they see the possibility of the fulfilment of their dreams by proxy through their child. They see their child as an extension of their own personality and project that child towards their own personal choice of vocation. Very often the child finds himself unhappily pursuing a vocation for which he is not equipped.

5. *Peer group.* During the teen years, one of the most powerful influences on our lives is our peer group, the friends we have and relate to. Very often opportunities for a meaningful vocation are squandered, because of this powerful influence which causes important years to be wasted, or

choices to be influenced by immature and foolish thinking.

6. *Inadequate opportunities.* When foresight is not given to a vocational choice, people may find that the training and education they have offers them very limited scope. John was like this. He graduated from university with a degree in Zoology. 'I don't really know what I want to do,' he said. 'I studied Zoology at university because I thought it would be interesting, but there aren't many opportunities in this field.'

Good vocational adjustment comes when we begin to consider the reason why we are inclining towards any given career. We discover the vocation for which we are best suited when we recognise that God has given us certain aptitudes and abilities, academic or practical, and when we evaluate these and work at developing them. God has committed himself to working with us to develop the abilities and talents that he has built into our lives. 'For I am confident of this very thing that he who hath begun a good work in you will perform it until the day of Christ Jesus' (Philippians 1.6). Paul is here confirming to the Philippians that God has made a tremendous investment in each of them, and is determined to bring that investment to fulfilment. We are not created and left to get along in the best way we can; God has given us abilities and aptitudes that with his help we can develop and channel for his purposes.

God's will

The most important aspect of vocational guidance is to seek God's will in the matter. But many people seem to have problems about this as they do not understand that there are two things to be borne in mind when considering God's will for their lives. One is service, that is, what we are to be doing for God and the other is character, that is, the kind of person we are. The most important aspect of our lives is that they carry the divine stamp of the character of God and portray his nature and likeness. Whatever we do in life we must do to the glory of God. This must be our basic commitment. When Jesus called his disciples he was committed first of all to refining their character. There are no short cuts to discovering the will of God for our lives, and before we can seek God concerning our vocation we must first seek him concerning his will to make us more Christlike and commit ourselves to that. When the vertical is right, then the rest works out. Relationship is the priority, then revelation comes. This is how it worked with Jesus. Let's examine some biblical principles for discovering God's will in our life.

Proverbs 3.5 and 6. 'Trust in the Lord with all thine heart; and lean not unto thine own understanding. In all thy ways acknowledge him, and he shall direct thy paths.' The question I usually ask people when counselling on this is: 'Have you obeyed everything God has shown you so far? If not, then God cannot take you on until you have obeyed in the area which has already been shown.' As we obey what God has shown us, then he will reveal the next step.

Then there is the area of sensitivity. How sensitive are you to what God is saying. Developing a sensitivity to God's voice, saying 'This is the way; walk ye in it' is done in the following ways.

Personal prayer: When we realise how much of his life Jesus gave to prayer there is no real difficulty in seeing why he was so confident concerning the will of God. 'My meat is to do the will of him that sent me.' 'If any man willeth to do his will he shall know of his teaching.'

Through constant communion with God our spirits become widened to the gentle pressures of the Holy Spirit by which we receive clear guidance.

Fasting: Those whom God has used greatly in Christian service have recognised the importance of reinforcing prayer with a period of fasting. Fasting means abstaining from eating, for the purpose of seeking God. It was common in Christ's day and was continued in the Early Church (Matthew 3.14; Acts 27.9). Spiritual perception increases if this is practised from time to time.

Meditation: Some Christians, when faced with a major decision, enter into a twenty-four hour fast in which the principles of biblical meditation are applied, along with fasting, to produce a clear mind on which decisions can be built. This is done by beginning to fast in the evening, by reading as much of the Scriptures as possible, then going to sleep with the Word of God resting very much upon your mind. On awakening in the morning, time is spent in prayer and communion with the Lord, together with further meditation in his Word. In this way Christians prepare themselves for the moment of clear direction which may come later in the day.

Then we must be willing to lay down our own ideas and desires. Often our approach is, 'Lord, this is what I want . . .', but it should be, 'Lord, I lay aside my own will in order to receive yours. If your will is the same as my will then that's fine, but if your will is different to mine . . . that's fine too.' This way we can take a step at a time. This is a principle which is illustrated by the Psalmist, who said, 'Thy Word is a lamp unto my feet and a light unto my path' (Psalm 119.105). God's Word is a lamp, not a floodlight. When we move a step at a time, then the light shines on the next step.

In a certain harbour in Europe, ships can only enter when the local pilot is allowed to board outside the harbour and bring in the ship under his personal control. Three lights in the harbour have to be seen as one before a safe entrance can be achieved. God's three harbour lights are as follows: the Word of God, the witness of the Spirit, circumstances. If a choice is to be made and one is not sure of the direction, then the alternative paths can be travelled prayerfully in the imagination. Providing prayer has been made (and perhaps fasting) then the mind will be ready to receive God's impressions.

Some Christians resort to the use of a 'fleece' to determine the will of God in their lives, basing this on the experience of Gideon in the book of Judges. A close examination of this incident will reveal that he used the 'fleece' not to determine the will of God, but to only confirm it.

Great care must be taken about discovering the will of God through the ministry of the gifts of the Spirit as outlined in 1 Corinthians 12. There should always be an inner witness to an outward voice. See Acts 15.28, 'It seemed good to the Holy Ghost *and to us.*'

Choosing a vocation

The choice of a specific vocation is not an easy task, as the possibilities are numerous. God created us to be achievers, to reach a destination, to attain a goal. Paul was clearly aware of this: 'Brethren, I count not myself to have apprehended: but this one thing I do, forgetting those things which are behind, and reaching forth unto those things which are before, I press toward the mark for the prize of the high calling of God in Christ Jesus' (Philippians 3.13–14). There was a sense of destiny and purpose about his life; he knew in which direction he was going. Many never achieve goals in their life, because they never take time prayerfully to establish them. According to David Schwartz, a goal is more than a dream. It is a dream being acted upon. It is more than a hazy, 'Oh, I wish that I could . . .', a goal is a clear, 'This is what I am working towards.' If we do not establish clear goals, then we will drift through life.

So, if we are to discover our life's vocation we must be prepared to examine the main areas of our life to see what our goals are. The best way to do this is write them down on a sheet of paper, and ask the question, 'What does God want me to accomplish in the next few years?' Overleaf is a chart to help you to do this. Follow it carefully and begin to consider what you are already doing with your life and what direction it is going in. Examine the seven areas listed and prayerfully consider your own goals in each area.

Once you have prayerfully established realistic goals and objectives you can begin to assess your natural aptitudes and abilities. An aptitude is a general ability to learn and perform a given task effectively. The question to ask is, 'What strength has God placed into my life that he wants me to develop and use?' It is important to recognise that in God's eyes all labour has equal merit, there are no superior, or inferior aptitudes, just different ones. The work of a carpenter is just as noble to God as that of a brain surgeon. It is society's interpretation of vocation that has demeaned some tasks and exalted others. Jesus illustrates this in the parable of the talents (Matthew 25.14–30). He did not expect the servant who only had one talent to out-produce the one who had five but simply charged each servant with a responsibility consistent with his ability. He was not concerned with who had made the highest return, but with what they had done with their resources. Each of us has a different quantity and combination of talents and abilities, and God simply wants us to develop the capabilities that we have. We are not to strive for positions that society has exalted or despise those it has denigrated. We are to pursue those areas of vocation that are consistent with our God-given capacities and capabilities. Although we may have several natural abilities there are usually one or two areas that will stand out more than others. It is good in the early stages of consideration to assess realistically whether or not our aptitudes are primarily practical or intellectual. The best way prayerfully to consider this is to take a personal evaluation which will highlight our strengths and weaknesses. We all have varying levels of intellect – the ability to acquire, assimilate, understand and interpret information received, and act upon it – which are determined by heredity, environment, education, etc. But this should not hinder us from using and developing the intellectual ability that we do have, by reading, thinking, learning through experience, talking with others. Many people who have not been rated with a high intelligence have achieved great things with their lives. They simply used all the ability and intelligence that God had given to

Sample goal chart

Area of life	Possible Goals	Possible Obstacles	Possible Solutions	Possible Rewards	Personal Praise
Intellectual	Increase my reading of Christian books (2 Tim. 2,15) To study the development & improvement of my ability to speak in public (Prov. 25, 11)	Not enough time I am a slow reader Lack of education Retiring disposition	Set aside time Take a reading course Enrol for an evening Adult Education Course Correspondence Course in Public Speaking	A more creative, interesting person A better conversationalist A positive influence in the lives of others	Example: I thank You Lord for a better understanding of Your Word, and a greater ability to share it with others
Emotional	To reduce stress and anxiety (Phil. 4,6 Phillips) To find real fulfillment (Acts 22,14)	Too much to do Schedule is too hectic No time to relax	Cut down schedule Make time to be alone and relax Seek professional help	A more relaxed person who is better able to cope with everyday situations	Example: I praise You, God for more inner peace and harmony
Physical	To lose weight To develop better health habits (1 Cor. 16,19–20)	I love to eat My work keeps me from adequate sleep and exercise	Self discipline Eat the right foods Revise schedule to include recreational activities	A healthier body Contributing to a more positive sense of well-being	Example: I am grateful for renewed energy with which to serve you

Spiritual	To be more Christ-like in my attitudes and activities (Rom. 8,29 TLB) (Gal. 2,20)	I soon get angry I am lacking in *genuine* love	Memorize 1 Peter 2 v 23 and quote it to myself before reacting Meditate more frequently on the fact that Christ has forgiven me	A deeper sense of Christ's presence and character being worked out through me	Example: Thank You Lord for a closer walk with You, and the increased awareness of Your presence
Family	To establish family devotions To spend more time together as a family (Prov. 22,6) (Psalm 127)	Family members have different time schedules Dissimilar interests	Have evening instead of morning devotions Open family discussions to establish a project of mutual interest	More emotional and spiritual unity and stability within the family	Example: Thank You Lord for bringing our family closer together
Financial	To pay my bills (Rom. 13,8) To tithe regularly (2 Cor. 9,7) To educate myself in financial matters (1 Cor. 4,2)	Low salary I spent too much I do not know where to seek advice	Establish a budget and stick to it Improve my abilities for a better job potential Ask at my local Christian bookshop for materials on the subject	Freedom from debt Improved family stability Having more to give to the work of God	Example: Thank You Lord for meeting my needs and enabling me to give to others
Social	Be a better friend Be sensitive to the needs of others (Rom. 12,10) Better role in community (Rom. 13)	I am too shy I don't know enough about local affairs I am too self-centred	Begin with simple kindnesses to friends Work at becoming involved in people's problems	Both my friends and I will be happier I am helping to build a better community	Example: Thank You Lord for enabling me to understand and help others

Personal goal chart – a regular review is essential for effectiveness

Area of life	Possible Goals	Possible Obstacles	Possible Solutions	Possible Rewards	Progress Made	Personal Praise
Intellectual						
Emotional						
Physical						

Spiritual						
Family						
Financial						
Social						

them. It's what we do with what God has given us that matters. It is therefore important to assess the level of our intelligence realistically and prayerfully. Is it average – above average – below average? Most of us will be able to judge this by how we found school, and by whether we find it difficult to grasp and understand things. This will help us to evaluate our intellectual potential along with our natural and more practical aptitudes. Assessing practical skills is of major importance as some are more suited to work with their hands. They have an ability to be creative and skilful by using the physical gifts with which God has blessed them.

Another key factor, in addition to discovering some goals for our lives and evaluating our aptitudes and intelligence, is identifying where our interests lie. Many people become unhappy in their jobs, and find no job satisfaction or fulfilment, because they are doing a job in which they have no interest. People who are interested in their work become contented and fulfilled in what they are doing, which affects every area of their life. Of course, interest alone does not form sufficient grounds on which to base our choice of a vocation. That interest must be consistent with our academic abilities and natural aptitudes. It is no good pursuing the vocation of a journalist because we are interested in it if we cannot spell and have failed all of our English exams. In considering a vocational choice, interest, aptitude, intelligence and clear realistic goals must be taken into account and brought to the Lord for his guidance and direction. We should discover the vocation that God has suited and equipped us for.

To summarise, therefore, the choice of a vocation will determine the quality of your future life, of your personal fulfilment, the use of your time, your earning capacity, job satisfaction, security, the stability of your family relationships, your christian witness and walk with God. As you begin to consider your vocation it will help you to recognise that God has given you natural abilities and you should prayerfully consider how you can best put them to use. Rather than allowing circumstances to dictate your vocation and role in life you should consider what realistic job opportunities are open to you so that you can make the choice. It also will help you to make wise selections of subjects to study and courses and qualifications to pursue as it is important to pursue training courses that are appropriate to your academic ability. In the following pages there are a series of exercises that are designed to help you to prayerfully consider the direction God is leading you in your life.

A General Personal Profile

Consider the following factors and write the answers on a separate sheet of paper. This will begin to help you to see a general profile of yourself:

Things I enjoy doing
Things I dislike doing
Qualifications I have achieved (or am studying for)
Activities I am involved in
What hobbies do I have?
Vocations that interest me
What do I have experience in?
What job am I currently doing?
Does it give job satisfaction?
Academic abilities
Practical skills
What previous jobs have I done?
What do I consider my abilities to be?
Conclusion: what have I learned about myself?

My personality evaluation

These are characteristics and traits that have become part of your personality. The objective here is not to evaluate them individually but to identify them, so that a vocation may be chosen that is compatible with your strengths.

Easygoing	☐	Adaptable	☐
Disciplined	☐	Flexible	☐
Friendly	☐	Competitive	☐
Good conversationalist	☐	Creative	☐
		Outgoing	☐
Caring	☐	Active	☐
Tenacious	☐	Imaginative	☐
Enjoy people	☐	Take initiative	☐
Like to be alone	☐	Introvert	☐
Honest	☐	Extrovert	☐
Practical	☐	Placid	☐
Tolerant	☐	Other	
Eye for detail	☐	Other	
Methodical	☐	Other	

It would be helpful to discuss your conclusions with those who know you well so that you can check that an accurate assessment has been made.

Aptitude inventory

Our natural aptitudes are of the utmost importance, and once we identify them, we can see to which type of vocation they are best suited.

Academic

Specific subjects (list out)	☐	Languages	☐
		Sciences	☐
Planning	☐	Finance	☐
Writing	☐	Keeping detailed records	☐
Teaching	☐		
Figure work	☐	Bible Study	☐
Researching	☐	Business	☐
Studying	☐	Reading	☐
Analysing	☐		

Practical

Organising	☐	Mechanical	☐
Working with hands	☐	Electrical	☐
		Driving	☐

Carpentry	☐	Serving others	☐
Gardening	☐	Cleaning	☐
Public speaking	☐	Building	☐
Selling	☐	Publicity	☐
Cooking	☐	Painting	☐
Meeting people	☐	Working with children	☐
Telephone work	☐	Social occasions	☐
Typing	☐		

Artistic

Designing	☐	Sports	☐
Creating	☐	Drawing	☐
Musical	☐	Dancing	☐
Handicrafts	☐	Fashion	☐
Graphics	☐	Decorating	☐
Inventing	☐	Sculpture	☐
Drama	☐	Arrangements	☐
Singing	☐	Hairdressing	☐

Interests

Natural interests play a strong part in job satisfaction and fulfilment. Consider the following areas to discover where your basic interests lie.

	ENJOY	DO NOT ENJOY
People	________	________
Places	________	________
Travel	________	________
Sports	________	________
Food	________	________
Cars	________	________
Books	________	________
Politics	________	________
Religion	________	________
Plants	________	________
Business	________	________
World affairs	________	________
Clothing	________	________
Animals	________	________
Art	________	________
Water sport	________	________
Photography	________	________
Country	________	________
Town	________	________
Reading	________	________
Gardening	________	________
Entertaining	________	________
Mixing socially	________	________
Needlework	________	________

Collecting things	______	______
Model making	______	______
Nature	______	______
Other		
Other		
Other		
Other		

We must now take our aptitudes, abilities and interests and put them together, so that we begin to gain a picture of the general type of vocation we would be best suited for.

Summary of factors from the three previous pages

1. Goals ____________________________
____
____
____

   Conclusion ________________________
____

2. Personality evaluation ________________
____
____
____

   Conclusion ________________________
____

3. Aptitude inventory ______________________

____

____

____

Conclusion ______________________

____

4. Interests ______________________

____

____

____

Conclusion ______________________

____

Overall conclusion

____

____

____

Based on the information recorded on the previous pages, select the vocation(s) that would be your preference, for which you feel you would be best suited and towards which you are most drawn. This is not a comprehensive list. It is important that you think of other areas of employment that you can add to it.

Possible jobs

Scientist	☐	Retailing Assistant	☐
Journalist	☐	Industrial Chemist	☐
Veterinary Surgeon	☐	Commercial Artist	☐
Educational Psychologist	☐	Despatch Clerk	☐
Biologist	☐	Publicity Officer	☐
Photographer	☐	Interviewer	☐
Insurance Clerk	☐	Social Worker	☐
Magazine Writer	☐	Minister of Religion	☐
Mathematics Teacher	☐	House Painter	☐
Pharmacist (Chemist)	☐	Motor Mechanic	☐
Youth Club Worker	☐	Commercial Traveller	☐
X-ray Therapist	☐	Bank Cashier	☐
Physiotherapist	☐	Postal Clerk	☐
Secretary	☐	Book-keeper	☐
Driver	☐	Advertising Executive	☐
Farmer	☐	Estate Agent	☐
Horticulturalist	☐	Solicitor	☐
Dental Assistant	☐	Caterer	☐
Hairdresser	☐	Cook	☐
Draughtsman	☐	Receptionist	☐
		Telephone Salesman	☐

Salesman	☐	Stockbroker	☐
Bank Manager	☐	Vet	☐
Carpenter	☐	Fashion Designer	☐
Doctor	☐	Commercial Artist	☐
Librarian	☐	Analyst	☐
Cashier	☐	Computer Programmer	☐
Plumber	☐	Civil Servant	☐
Electrician	☐	Transport Worker	☐
Nurse	☐	Other	
Teacher	☐	Other	
Builder	☐	Other	
Accounts Clerk	☐		
Printer	☐		

List the five occupations in order of choice that you would most like to pursue.

1. ______________________________

2. ______________________________

3. ______________________________

4. ______________________________

5. ______________________________

From these exercises you will begin to see where your aptitudes, interests and strengths lie and how they interrelate. You will need to find out the types of employment where they can be best applied. Once you begin to decide on the type of job you would like to pursue, you will need to research the qualities and abilities needed for it. In this way you can begin to match together vocational possibilities with your own capabilities. The next step is to see what is required in terms of training and qualifications to secure that job, and how you can follow the necessary course to obtain those qualifications. This can be done by considering the following possibilities.

C.S.E., O Levels, Polytech/A level/University/specialised training/day release. If your choice for a vocation begins to emerge while you are still at school, it would be helpful to see if you could find a part-time summer job in that area. It is also helpful to talk to those who are already actively engaged in that vocation, so that they can reflect to you all its involvements and answer your questions.

Once we begin to discover the area of vocation that is God's choosing for our life, we must realistically consider the opportunities that are open to us. This can be done in a number of ways: chatting with the careers guidance officer; visiting the local employment office, and employment bureau; watching the local press; writing to local firms; considering the possibility of moving to another area; and also by letting your friends know that you are looking for an opening in that particular sphere. Once your thinking is beginning to crystallise it is good to seek wise and sound counsel from a godly minister, or from those who have your spiritual interest at heart.

You may want to consider the possibility of pursuing a vocation within a christian organisation as part of your christian commitment and service. The term 'full time' christian service is often used for those who are working for christian organisations or churches, but whether we are called to work in a secular or christian context we are all called to be in 'full time' christian service.

You may feel that God is calling you to the ministry or for service as a missionary, in which case you will need to spend a period of time in preparation, and the best place undoubtedly is at a bible or theological college. Although this is not a necessity, most mission organisations and denominations will require an adequate period of training. Many christian organisations and mission societies have needs for specialised skills and trained help so that they can effectively carry out the work that God has called them to do. These include such areas as secretarial and clerical work, administration, management, accounts, publishing, graphic art, computer programming, and public relations. A letter to christian organisations, mission societies, publishers, and church denominations will begin to show you the vocational opportunities that are available. Many Christian organisations and societies are hampered in their work because they cannot find the trained personnel who are committed Christians.

It could be that you are already in a vocation, but have not been overly successful and feel a sense of vocational failure. Maybe this is because of one of the reasons mentioned earlier. You need to use these exercises prayerfully to re-appraise the direction of your life.

Vocational dangers

When choosing a vocation there are a number of dangers that we must try to avoid. Sometimes people are motivated to choose a vocation because of deep insecurities in their life, and out of a need to prove to themselves and others that they are able to be successful. They become what is known as workoholics.

The old adage 'Hard work never killed anyone' may be true but it is not true that 'Too much hard work never killed anyone.' The syndrome known as workoholism is becoming more and more familiar in our society and in church circles. It is the inner drive and compulsion to push oneself to the point of physical and mental exhaustion. Of course we must always strive for a standard of excellence, and show diligence in our work, but the workoholic is driven beyond his limits. Often people involved in christian work are workoholics although they do not realise it. They are trying to earn God's love by what they do. The truth is that God loves us for who we are, not what we do. We must learn to rest in his love, and learn to say NO to the many demands that are placed on us. It is important that we rest in the security of God's purpose for our life rather than striving to find security through our career. Our vocation should always be our servant and not our master.

One of the reasons why we over-exert ourselves in our vocation is that we have never learned how to utilise properly the time that is available to us. So often we say 'How time flies' and yet really we know that time is constant, it's just that we never seem to have enough of it because we are doing so much. Time is a sacred trust given to us by God, to use wisely and conscientiously. Often we do not make the best use of our time because we do not establish and follow the right priorities. We become involved in pursuing things that take our time and yet are relatively unimportant. Until we stop and sort out the multiplicity of tasks, we will always be running ourselves ragged, doing a lot but accomplishing little.

The best way to work through this problem is to take stock and evaluate just where our time is being spent, so we can then plan ahead to make better use of our time. To help you do this, I have put a time chart (p. 52). It is a simple tool, but very effective if used properly and wisely. It covers a twenty-four hour period for the seven days of the week. Make a list of all the things you normally spend time on in an average week: sleeping – eating – working – family – church activities – prayer and bible study – leisure – gardening, etc. Once you have listed them out, fill in the amount of time you spend on each on the Time Chart. You will then begin to see where some of your problems lie. If you want to overcome them, make a fresh list but in order of priority and then re-schedule your time chart. It will take discipline to re-schedule your activities, but you must be firm with yourself, so that you are accomplishing the priorities that God has placed in your life. Charles E. Hummell in a small pamphlet entitled the *Tyranny of the Urgent*, points out that it is the urgent task which seemingly has to be done right now which causes us to keep going at a frenetic pace, and prevents us from doing the more important task which God desires us to achieve. We must therefore learn to differentiate between the urgent and the important. The urgent tasks may be important to us, but we must be strong enough to withstand their pressures and achieve the right priorities. Before you can be free to manage your time wisely, you must first of all learn to manage yourself.

As all behaviour springs from inner motives,

we must ask ourselves why it is that we get caught up in the workoholic syndrome.

One reason could be that we are attempting to run from our inner selves. We know that busy people get much accomplished, and receive praise for what they accomplish, but we could be using the pressure to hide our feelings of failure and inadequacy. As long as we are busy we tend to feel good about ourselves, but as soon as we slow down, doubts begin to arise about our self-worth. It is possible that we grew up in a home where achievement meant love and acceptance, and where failure meant rejection and disgrace. As a result we developed a pattern of trying to earn love and approval by the amount of work we accomplished. Maybe we come from a family background where we were made to feel useless, and now we are going through life trying to prove through what we do that we are useful. As adults we continue to be concerned about what others are thinking. We reason thus – 'Maybe they'll think I am lazy if I don't keep going' or 'I need to make a good impression so I'll keep busy.'

Another reason could be that we are easily bored with details. Some of us see ourselves achieving big things, but find no interest or sense of achievement with practical details. We tend

A time chart

An examination of my weekly schedule for the week commencing ....

Name .... Age ....

The purpose of the chart is to enable you to decide the best use of your time.
Fill in the spaces, indicating exactly what you did for each hour period.
It is important to record *what you did*, not what you intended to do or should have done.

HOURS	MON	TUES	WED	THURS	FRI	SAT	SUN
AM 12–5							
5–6							
6–7							
7–8							
8–9							
9–10							
10–11							
11–12							

PM 12–1							
1–2							
2–3							
3–4							
4–5							
5–6							
6–7							
7–8							
8–9							
9–10							
10–11							
11–12							

'Make the best use of your time, despite all the evils of these days. Don't be vague but grasp firmly what you know to be the will of the Lord.' *Ephesians 5.16–17 (Phillips)* then to concentrate on big tasks and let others handle the details, working ourselves into bigger and bigger projects that will occupy our whole attention.

It could also be that we are avoiding close relationships. A young girl, whenever she was at a social occasion, made sure she was involved in serving and helping so that she would avoid any close personal contact with people. Keeping busy was her way of avoiding trying to say something important and interesting, and then feeling she had said the wrong thing.

Very often accompanying the workoholic syndrome is the perfectionist syndrome: everything must be spot on. This is caused by deep feelings of insecurity that if we do not achieve the highest standard we will not be accepted.

There is scientific evidence to show that perpetual busyness, while it may help us to get a lot done, also takes a heavy toll. Our vocation becomes a hard taskmaster, driving us on so that we lose all sense of personal identity, finding significance only in what we do.

It takes its toll physically in building up tension in our bodies, that finally shows itself in stomach ulcers, blood pressure, asthma, migraine headaches, etc. Busyness also takes its toll psychologically in upsetting the emotional balance of our lives, creating irritation, tension, and other disorders. It affects us spiritually in getting us to drop out of our scheduled important periods of spiritual enrichment. Someone said, 'If we are too busy to pray, or read our Bibles, then we are busier than God intended us to be.'

The starting point for breaking out of this constant pressure of work is to identify the reasons for it. We must ask ourselves:

Am I running from deep involvement with others?
Do I always have to be on the go to gain a sense of self worth?
Is it because I have not learned to organise my day?
Are there any other 'hidden' reasons?

Once the cause for our constant involvement in activity and work becomes apparent we are in a better position to reject its controlling and pushing power.

1. *Differentiate between the urgent and the important.* Many demands made upon us, although urgent, may not be important. We must learn to evaluate our priorities. All too often we major in

the minors and minor in the majors. We let important things detract from the *most* important, or the good things from the best. Let's put first things first, and omit lesser things and really find God's priorities for our lives.

2. *Discover the secret of Christ's perfect poise.* A clue is given in Mark's Gospel where, after an extremely busy day, 'in the morning a great while before day. He (Jesus) rose and went out to a lonely place, and there he prayed' (Mark 1.35). Jesus had no divinely drawn blueprint which he followed, but discerned his Father's will day by day through personal prayer.

3. *Reserve a few minutes each day to take stock of your life.* Regularly evaluate your use of time, and plan your activities so that you are achieving maximum effectiveness with minimum weariness. When God told man to rest every seventh day, perhaps it was to enable him to evaluate his priorities and not merely immerse himself in the frenzied Sunday programmes which characterise the 'day of rest' for so many people.

4. *Don't blame your busyness on external circumstances.* We say such things as 'I've got to – so and so is depending on me' or 'I can't because I

don't have time.' There is comparatively little that we *really* have to do. We must be ready to make clear decisions about what we should be doing and what we should not be doing. If we slow down long enough to listen to God, we might find that he would have us cut out some committee meetings, or other 'important' activities, so as to concentrate on other areas in a more meaningful way.

5. *Place your whole being in God's perspective.* See yourself as a central part of God's creation, and realise that when caught up in the wheels of destiny, no one that belongs to Christ need ever feel anxious, worried or afraid. Let go your desire to fit every conceivable activity into your day, and simply let God make clear to you the wisest and most prudent use of your time. As we allow God to control our lives and surrender to him every part of our being, he will give us the strength and insight to plan our activities in a more constructive way.

6. *Delegate some tasks to others.* 'And Jesus said unto them, "Come ye after me and I will make you fishers of men" ' (Mark 1.17). Even though Jesus was the Son of God, he still saw the neces-

sity of delegating responsibility to others in order that he might achieve his goals.

Robert Coleman in *The Master Plan of Evangelism* says that in order to get the most out of our time we should:

(a) Eliminate unessential activities
(b) Speed up essential activities
(c) Delegate some tasks to others.

One of the most interesting challenges to using our time correctly is to sit down and work out how others can best take over our efforts. Can letters be typed by someone else? Is it possible that someone else can do or perform tasks as effectively as us, leaving our time free for more essential details?

7. *Take time off for rest and relaxation.* 'And in the morning, rising up a great while before the day, Jesus went out and departed into a solitary place, and there prayed' (Mark 1.35). Later, he said to his disciples, 'Come ye yourselves apart and rest awhile' (Mark 6.31). In addition to time for quiet prayer and meditation, we need time for rest and relaxation. We will never learn to make effective use of our time until we know how to detach ourselves from what we are doing at

appropriate occasions, and give ourselves to relaxation and recreation.

Our spiritual, psychological and physical development will be greatly hindered if we become slaves to our work. The word 'recreation' really means 're-creation' when our bodies, minds and spirits become re-created as we relax and rest or become involved in other less strenuous activities.

Even the Puritan pastor, Benjamin Colman, back in 1707, when leisure was considered to be unspiritual and unnecessary, wrote 'We daily need some respite and diversion, without which we dull our power. It spoils the bow to always keep it bent.'

Each one of us has exactly the amount of time needed to complete the task which God has set for us before time began. God has a specific and unique design for every life and seeks, as he did with Jesus, to bring to perfection a particular purpose which is unique to every single individual. We must not squander minutes on self-centred activities, and then get caught up in a hurry syndrome to squeeze out the extra energy we need to compensate for our lack of divine direction.

Remember, you can't meet every need that is

going to present itself to you, so don't try. Consider what God wants you to do in every situation and don't be browbeaten into accepting responsibilities which God never intends you to have.

Another vocational danger is the exact opposite of the danger of overwork: we often work to less than our potential and feel frustrated because we are under-employed. The reason can be that we are unable to move any further in our vocation, because there has been inadequate or insufficient preparation and qualifications. Shortcuts taken in preparation for a vocation are going to reveal themselves at some stage when it may be too late to retrace our steps and gain the required qualifications. It is always wise to take as much training as is possible in the earlier years of a vocation so that one's full potential and capacity can be utilised. John was like this when he came to see me. He was frustrated in his job because he could go no further, yet he had not maximised his full job potential. Fortunately he was able to study at evening classes although he found it hard with a wife and two small children. After a year's hard work, he was able to change his job to one that had added responsibility in which he could use his full potential.

Then there is the danger of wrong promotion.

In his best selling book *The Peter Principle*, Dr Laurence J. Peter, makes the observation, 'that a man tends to rise in an organisational hierarchy to the level of his own incompetence.' What he means by this is that often people are promoted in their vocation to a position that they cannot cope with and in which they feel inadequate. The opportunity for advancement is presented to them with a higher salary, but when they get into their new positions they find that the demands and responsibilities are too much for them, and they begin to work under much stress and strain and duress. They become incompetent in their new position and this then affects every area of their life. We must be willing to recognise our limits, and not overreach ourselves. It's possible to find ourselves in this position because of the inducements and advantages that go with the new job. Prestige and a higher salary should never be our motivation for advancement. Priority must always be placed on God's will and purpose, and he will never allow us to get into a position where we are living under stress, anxiety and duress. In an age of materialism, Satan often uses this trap to sap the effectiveness of the lives of God's people.

Several years ago a vocational guidance pilot

scheme was set up by the Crusade for World Revival, to help Christians discover their God-given potential and their natural and spiritual gifts in order to pursue God's purpose for their lives. This scheme puts together three comprehensive forms of analysis: (a) discovering your basic gift (see p. 32 of *Discovering Your Place in the Body of Christ*); (b) the Taylor-Johnson temperament analysis; (c) the Rothwell Miller questionnaire. With these, and with prayer for God's guidance, men and women from a wide spectrum of the christian population have been counselled about their vocation. Follow-up two years later on several who have undergone guidance has shown that counsellees who have in general put into effect the guidance given have found themselves fulfilled in what they now believe is God's vocation for them.[1] The most important lesson that has been learned from this pilot scheme is that christian vocational guidance is of the utmost importance.

Although the exercises in this booklet are not exhaustive, if you use them wisely and properly, they will help to focus your attention on God's vocational purposes for your life.

[1]C.W.R. have been careful, to date, not to advertise this service widely as the number of counsellors available is limited.